D1180319

C.S.LEWIS

~ on ~

GRIEF

C.S. LEWIS

~ *on* ~

GRIEF

*Compiled by*

LESLEY WALMSLEY

HarperCollins*Publishers*

HarperCollins*Publishers*
77–85 Fulham Palace Road, London W6 8JB

First published in Great Britain
in 1998 by HarperCollins*Publishers*

1 3 5 7 9 10 8 6 4 2

Extracts from C.S. Lewis's works © C.S. Lewis Pte Ltd.
Introduction and compilation © 1998 Lesley Walmsley
Cover illustration © 1998 Sarah Young

Produced for HarperCollins*Publishers* by Godsfield Press

*Designed and produced by*
THE BRIDGEWATER BOOK COMPANY LTD

Picture research by Jane Moore

A catalogue record for this book is
available from the British Library.

ISBN 0 00 628077 3

Printed in Hong Kong

CONDITIONS OF SALE

# Contents

# Introduction

rief can be described as a deep sorrow or distress. There is a great hurt in grief, generally a feeling that no one else really understands, that no one else has ever suffered in quite this way or to quite this extent. Whether anyone else really can understand

*C.S. Lewis*

properly exactly how you feel in your own personal grief may be open to question – how can anyone measure pain and suffering? – and we are all separate individuals. Perhaps you don't want to survive in your present anguish, but as the hours and the days go by, our minds and bodies adapt to whatever is the cause of our grief, and slowly we do realize that we are surviving. We shall never forget, but we shall cope.

One of the things that can help as you begin to crawl up from the worst depths of pain and suffering is to see how someone else has suffered and yet survived. The writings of C.S. Lewis, particularly A Grief Observed, written after the death of his beloved wife, Joy, have spoken to thousands in their own grief. Here is a highly intelligent and articulate man putting into words what maybe you have felt and so can recognize, the only kind of person who has the right to speak to you about grief because he is feeling it *himself. This is no calm approach by a skilled counsellor, but real feeling, real distress, real bewilderment at the fear, the lethargy, the self-pity of grief.*

Grief came first to Clive Staples (Jack) Lewis as a small boy in Belfast when his mother died, leaving his father to bring up him and his older brother Warren (Warnie). He met another kind of grief during his military service in the First World War. Above all Jack Lewis grieved for the early loss of Joy, the woman who, late in his life, brought him love and happiness and a special friendship, and with whom he spent a few truly joyful years.

Jack and Warnie

Jack was born in Belfast on 29 November 1898, and after his mother's death was sent to boarding school in England. In due course he went up to Oxford University, and began a brilliant academic career, being elected a Fellow of Magdalen College in 1925. He was also one of a group of writers, including J.R.R. Tolkien and Owen Barfield, known as The Inklings. They met in Lewis's rooms or in a pub called the Eagle and Child, at first on Monday mornings (soon moved to Tuesdays), and later on Thursday evenings as well. This carried on from about 1930 until Lewis's death in 1963. Some of this small group remained friends for the rest of their lives, and they were largely responsible for Jack's conversion to Christianity in 1931.

Jack Lewis had an incisive mind and, having argued against the teachings of Christianity in his time as an atheist, when he was converted he was able to marshal his beliefs equally clearly. One

*Oxford, from Headington Hill*

result of this was that the BBC asked him to give four radio talks during the Second World War on 'Right and Wrong'. These were such a success that more series followed, and eventually they were all published as Mere Christianity, *the best-selling and most popular of all his religious books.*

*Lewis was writing in a very different kind of world from the one in which we live today. In particular, as women were then only beginning to exert much influence outside the home, it was quite normal to refer to 'a man who', whereas today we would use more inclusive language. Lewis respected everyone for what they were, and if he were writing now this would be reflected in his style. But he is not, and I have decided to leave his thoughts as he expressed them.*

*Magdalen College*

*I hope that this selection of his writings will help you or anyone you know who may be struggling with grief to come through with hope and dignity.*

≈ *LESLEY WALMSLEY*

# Epitaph for
# Helen Joy Davidman

*Remember*
HELEN JOY
DAVIDMAN

*D. July 1960*
*Loved wife of C.S. Lewis*

*Here the whole world (stars, water, air*
*And field, and forest, as they were*
*Reflected in a single mind)*
*Like cast-off clothes was left behind*
*In ashes yet with hope that she,*
*Re-born from holy poverty,*
*In lenten lands, hereafter may*
*Resume them on her Easter Day.*

≈ *POEMS*

# When the house is empty

No one ever told me that grief felt so like fear. I am not afraid, but the sensation is like being afraid. The same fluttering in the stomach, the same restlessness, the yawning. I keep on swallowing.

At other times it feels like being mildly drunk, or concussed. There is a sort of invisible blanket between the world and me. I find it hard to take in what anyone says. Or perhaps, hard to want to take it in. It is so uninteresting. Yet I want the others to be about me. I dread the moments when the house is empty. If only they would talk to one another and not to me…

There are moments, most unexpectedly, when something inside me tries to assure me that I don't really mind so much, not so very much, after all. Love is not the whole of a man's life. I was happy before I ever met H. I've plenty of what are called 'resources'… One is ashamed to listen to this voice but it seems for a little to be making out a good case. Then comes a sudden jab of red-hot memory and all this 'commonsense' vanishes like an ant in the mouth of a furnace…

And no one ever told me about the laziness of grief…
Not only writing but even reading a letter is too much.
Even shaving. What does it matter now whether my
cheek is rough or smooth? They say an unhappy man
wants distractions – something to take him out of
himself. Only as a dog-tired man wants an extra blanket
on a cold night; he'd rather lie there shivering than get
up and find one.

≈ *A GRIEF OBSERVED*

*The Empty House*, L.S. LOWRY (1887–1976)

# Count the cost

When I was a child I often had toothache, and I knew that if I went to my mother she would give me something which would deaden the pain for that night and let me get to sleep. But I did not go to my mother – at least, not till the pain became very bad... I did not doubt she would give me the aspirin; but I knew she would also do something else. I knew she would take me to the dentist next morning... I wanted immediate relief from pain: but I could not get it without having my teeth set permanently right. And I knew those dentists; I knew they started fiddling about with all sorts of other teeth which had not yet begun to ache...

Now, if I may put it that way, Our Lord is like the dentists.... Dozens of people go to Him to be cured of some one particular sin which they are ashamed of... or which is obviously spoiling daily life... Well, He will cure it all right: but He will not stop there. That may be all you asked: but if once you call Him in, He will give you the full treatment...

That is why He warned people to 'count the cost' before becoming Christians. 'Make no mistake,' He says, 'if you let me, I will make you perfect… Whatever suffering it may cost you in your earthly life, whatever inconceivable purification it may cost you after death, whatever it costs Me, I will never rest, nor let you rest, until you are literally perfect – until my Father can say without reservation that He is well pleased with you, as He said He was well pleased with me…'

And yet – this is the other and equally important side of it – this Helper who will, in the long run, be satisfied with nothing less than absolute perfection, will also be delighted with the first feeble, stumbling effort you make tomorrow to do the simplest duty.

≈ *MERE CHRISTIANITY*

*Angel with a Sword*
HANS MEMLING (FL.1465–95)

# Killed every day

Did you ever think, when you were a child, what fun it would be if your toys could come to life? Well, suppose you could really have brought them to life. Imagine turning a tin soldier into a real little man. It would involve turning the tin into flesh. And suppose the tin soldier did not like it. He is not interested in flesh; all he sees is that the tin is being spoilt. He thinks you are killing him...

What you would have done about that tin soldier I do not know. But what God did about us was this. The Second Person in God, the Son, became human Himself: was born into the world as an actual man – a real man of a particular height, with hair of a particular colour, speaking a particular language, weighing so many stone. The Eternal Being... became not only a man but (before that) a baby, and before that a foetus inside a woman's body. If you want to get the hang of it, think how you would like to become a slug or crab...

*The Morning of the Resurrection,* EDWARD BURNE-JONES (1833-98)

Thus in one instance humanity had... passed into the life of Christ. And because the whole difficulty for us is that the natural life has to be, in a sense, 'killed', he chose an earthly career which involved the killing of His human desires at every turn – poverty, misunderstanding from His own family, betrayal by one of His intimate friends, being jeered at and manhandled by the police, and execution by torture. And then, after being thus killed – killed every day in a sense – the human creature in Him, because it was united to the divine Son, came to life again. The Man in Christ rose again: not only the God. That is the whole point. For the first time we saw a real man. One tin soldier – real tin, just like the rest – had come fully and splendidly alive.

≈ *MERE CHRISTIANITY*

# Being an
# embarrassment

I cannot talk to the children about her. The moment I try, there appears on their faces neither grief, nor love, nor fear, nor pity, but the most fatal of all non-conductors, embarrassment. They look as if I were committing an indecency... I can't blame them. It's the way boys are...

Or are the boys right? What would H. herself think of this terrible little notebook to which I come back and back? Are these jottings morbid?... Part of every misery is, so to speak, the misery's shadow or reflection: the fact that you don't merely suffer but have to keep on thinking about the fact that you suffer. I not only live each endless day in grief, but live each day thinking about living each day in grief. Do these notes merely aggravate that side of it? Merely confirm the monotonous, treadmill march of the mind round one subject? But what am I to do? I must have some drug, and reading isn't a strong enough drug now...

An odd by-product of my loss is that I'm aware of being an embarrassment to everyone I meet. At work, at the club, in the street, I see people, as they approach me, trying to make up their minds whether they'll 'say something about it' or not. I hate it if they do, and if they don't... I like best the well-brought-up young men, almost boys, who walk up to me as if I were a dentist, turn very red, get it over, and then edge away to the bar as quickly as they decently can. Perhaps the bereaved ought to be isolated in special settlements like lepers.

To some I'm worse than an embarrassment. I am a death's head. Whenever I meet a happily married pair I can feel them both thinking, 'One or other of us must some day be as he is now.'

≈ *A GRIEF OBSERVED*

# Grief in childhood

For us boys the real bereavement had happened before our mother died... They say that a shared sorrow draws people closer together; I can hardly believe that it often has that effect when those who share it are of widely different ages... [My father's] nerves had never been of the steadiest and his emotions had always been uncontrolled. Under the pressure of anxiety his temper became incalculable; he spoke wildly and acted unjustly. Thus by a peculiar cruelty of fate, during those months the unfortunate man, had he but known it, was really losing his sons as well as his wife...

*Jack and his father, Albert, 1918*

Grief in childhood is complicated with many other miseries. I was taken into the bedroom where my mother lay dead; as they said, 'to see her', in reality, as I knew at once, 'to see it'. There was nothing that a grown-up would call disfigurement – except for that total disfigurement which is death itself. Grief was overwhelmed in terror. To this day I do not know what they mean when they call dead bodies beautiful. The ugliest man alive is an angel of beauty compared with the loveliest of the dead…

With my mother's death all settled happiness, all that was tranquil and reliable, disappeared from my life. There was to be much fun, many pleasures, many stabs of Joy; but no more of the old security. It was sea and islands now; the great continent had sunk like Atlantis.

≈ *SURPRISED BY JOY*

# Going to Hell

We have been through very deep waters. Mrs Moore's brother – the Doc – came here and had a sudden attack of war neurasthenia. He was here for nearly three weeks, and endured awful mental tortures. Anyone who didn't know would have mistaken it for lunacy – we did at first: he had horrible maniacal fits – had to be held down... He had the delusion that he was going to Hell...

The Doctor who came to see the Doc (a psychoanalyst and neurological specialist) said that every neurotic case *Oxford, 1944* went back to the childish fear of the father. But it can be avoided. Keep clear of introspection, of brooding, of spiritualism, of everything eccentric. Keep to work and sanity and open air... We hold our mental health by a thread: and nothing is worth risking it for. Above all beware of excessive day dreaming, of seeing yourself in the centre of a drama, of self-pity, and, as far as possible, of fears.

≈ *THEY STAND TOGETHER*

*The Small Last Judgement (detail)*
PETER PAUL RUBENS (1577–1640)

# Where is she now?

'Where is she now?'... Kind people have said to me, 'She is with God.' In one sense that is most certain. She is, like God, incomprehensible and unimaginable.

But I find that this question, however important it may be in itself, is not after all very important in relation to grief. Suppose that the earthly lives she and I shared for a few years are in reality only the basis for, or prelude to, or earthly appearance of, two unimaginable, super-cosmic, eternal somethings. Those somethings could be pictured as spheres or globes. Where the plane of Nature cuts through them – that is, in earthly life – they appear as two circles (circles are slices of spheres)... But those two circles, above all the point at which they touched, are the very thing I am mourning for, homesick for, famished for. You tell me 'she goes on'. But my heart and body are crying out, come back, come back. Be a circle, touching my circle on the plane of Nature...

I know that the thing I want is exactly the thing I can never get. The old life, the jokes, the drinks, the

*Othello and Desdemona (detail),*
THEODORE CHASSERIAU (1819–56)

arguments, the love-making, the tiny, heart-breaking commonplace... It is a part of the past. And the past is the past and that is what time means, and time itself is one more name for death, and Heaven itself is a state where 'the former things have passed away'...

Talk to me about the truth of religion and I'll listen gladly. Talk to me about the duty of religion and I'll listen submissively. But don't come talking to me about the consolations of religion or I shall suspect that you don't understand... Reality never repeats... That is what we should all like. The happy past restored.

And that, just that, is what I cry out for, with mad, midnight endearments and entreaties spoken into the empty air.

≈ *A GRIEF OBSERVED*

# Memory can
# transfigure

*Haweswater, Lake District,* CONSTANT-EMILE TROYON (1810–65)

Don't talk to me of the 'illusions' of memory. Why should what we see at the moment be more 'real' than what we see from ten years' distance? It is indeed an illusion to believe that the blue hills on the horizon would still look blue if you went to them. But the fact that they are blue five miles away, and the fact that they are green when you are on them, are equally good facts. Traherne's 'orient and immortal wheat' or Wordsworth's landscape 'apparelled in celestial light' may not have

been so radiant in the past when it was present as in the remembered past. That is the beginning of the glorification. One day they will be more radiant still. Thus in the sense-bodies of the redeemed the whole New Earth will arise. The same yet not the same as this. It was sown in corruption, it is raised in incorruption…

The strangest discovery of a widower's life is the possibility, sometimes, of recalling with detailed and uninhibited imagination, with tenderness and gratitude, a passage of carnal love, yet with no re-awakening of concupiscence. And when this occurs (it must not be sought) awe comes upon us. It is like seeing Nature itself rising from the grave. What was  sown in momentariness is raised in still permanence. What was sown as a becoming rises as being. Sown in subjectivity, it rises in objectivity. The transitory secret of two is now a chord in the ultimate music.

≈ *PRAYER: LETTERS TO MALCOLM*

# This dead flatness

It's not true that I'm always thinking of H. Work and conversation make that impossible. But the times when I'm not are perhaps my worst. For then, though I have forgotten the reason, there is spread over everything a vague sense of wrongness, of something amiss. Like in those dreams where nothing terrible occurs – nothing that would sound even remarkable if you told it at breakfast time – but the atmosphere, the taste, of the whole thing is deadly. So with this. I see the rowan berries reddening and don't know for a moment why they, of all things, should be depressing. I hear a clock strike and some quality it always had before has gone out of the sound. What's wrong with the world to make it so flat, shabby, worn-out looking? Then I remember…

Feelings, and feelings, and feelings. Let me try thinking instead... I knew already that these things, and worse, happened daily. I would have said that I had taken them into account. I had been warned – I had warned myself – not to reckon on worldly happiness. We were even promised sufferings. They were part of the programme. We were even told 'Blessed are they that mourn,' and I accepted it. I've got nothing that I hadn't bargained for. Of course it is different when the thing happens to oneself, not to others, and in reality, not in imagination...

≈ *A GRIEF OBSERVED*

# The darkness outside

I notice that Our Lord, while stressing the terror of Hell with unsparing severity, usually emphasizes the idea not of duration but of *finality*. Consignment to the consuming fire is usually treated as the end of the story – not as the beginning of a new story. That the lost soul is eternally fixed in its diabolical attitude we cannot doubt:

*The Mocking of Christ,*
MATTIAS GRUNEWALD (1455–1528)

but whether this eternal fixity implies endless duration – or duration at all – we cannot say... We know much more about Heaven than Hell, for Heaven is the home of humanity and therefore contains all that is implied in a glorified human life: but Hell was not made

for men. It is in no sense *parallel* to Heaven: it is 'the darkness outside', the outer rim where being fades away into nonentity...

In the long run the answer to all those who object to the doctrine of Hell, is itself a question: 'What are you asking God to do?' To wipe out their past sins and, at all costs, to give them a fresh start, smoothing every difficulty and offering every miraculous help? But He has done so, on Calvary. To forgive them? They will not be forgiven. To leave them alone? Alas, I am afraid that is what He does...

In all discussions of Hell we should keep steadily before our eyes the possible damnation, not of our enemies nor our friends (since both these disturb the reason) but of ourselves. This chapter is not about your wife or son, nor about Nero or Judas Iscariot; it is about you and me.

≈ *THE PROBLEM OF PAIN*

# The evil of pain

'If God were good, He would wish to make His creatures perfectly happy, and if God were almighty He would be able to do what He wished. But the creatures are not happy. Therefore God lacks either goodness, or power, or both.' This is the problem of pain, in its simplest form…

*Agony in the Garden*, ANDREA MANTEGNA (1431–1506)

If matter has a fixed nature and obeys constant laws, not all states of matter will be equally agreeable to the wishes of a given soul, nor all equally beneficial for that particular aggregate of matter which he calls his body. If fire comforts that body at a certain distance, it will destroy it when the distance is reduced. Hence, even in a perfect world, the necessity for those danger

*C.S. Lewis, 1938*

signals which the pain-fibres in our nerves are apparently designed to transmit. Does this mean an inevitable element of evil (in the form of pain) in any possible world? I think not: for while it may be true that the least sin is an incalculable evil, the evil of pain depends on degree, and pains below a certain intensity are not feared or resented at all. No one minds the process 'warm – beautifully hot – too hot – it stings' which warns him to withdraw his hand from exposure to the fire: and, if I may trust my own feeling, a slight aching in the legs as we climb into bed after a good day's walking is, in fact, pleasurable.

≈ *THE PROBLEM OF PAIN*

# Is it not yet enough?

What is grief compared with physical pain? Whatever fools may say, the body can suffer twenty times more than the mind. The mind has always some power of evasion. At worst, the unbearable thought only comes back and back, but the physical pain can be absolutely continuous. Grief is like a bomber circling round and dropping its bombs each time the circle brings it overhead; physical pain is like the steady barrage on a trench in World War One, hours of it with no let-up for a moment. Thought is never static; pain often is…

What sort of a lover am I to think so much about my affliction and so much less about hers? Even the insane call, 'Come back,' is all for my own sake. I never even raised the question whether such a return, if it were possible, would be good for her. I want her back as an ingredient in the restoration of *my* past. Could I have wished her anything worse? Having got once through death, to come back and then, at some later date, have all her dying to do over again?…

*December 30th 1940–again tonight?*, DAVID SHEPHERD

My love for H. was of much the same quality as my faith in God... But neither was the thing I thought it was. A good deal of the card-castle about both...

H. was a splendid thing; a soul straight, bright, and tempered like a sword. But not a perfected saint. A sinful woman married to a sinful man; two of God's patients, not yet cured. I know there are not only tears to be dried but stains to be scoured. The sword will be made even brighter.

But, oh God, tenderly, tenderly. Already, month by month and week by week you broke her body on the wheel whilst she still wore it. Is it not yet enough?

≈ *A GRIEF OBSERVED*

# Pain as God's megaphone

*The Eleventh Hour, the Eleventh Day of the Eleventh Month, 1918,*
W. PERCY DAY (FL. 1905–22)

God whispers to us in our pleasures, speaks in our conscience, but shouts in our pain: it is His megaphone to rouse a deaf world…

When our ancestors referred to pains and sorrows as God's 'vengeance' upon sin they were not necessarily attributing evil passions to God; they may have been recognizing the good element in the idea of retribution.

Until the evil man finds evil unmistakably present in his existence, in the form of pain, he is enclosed in illusion. Once pain has roused him, he knows that he is in some way or other 'up against' the real universe: he either rebels... or else makes some attempt at an adjustment, which, if pursued, will lead him to religion...

Everyone has noticed how hard it is to turn our thoughts to God when everything is going well with us... What then can God do in our interests but make 'our own life' less agreeable to us?... We are perplexed to see misfortune falling upon decent, inoffensive, worthy people... How can I say with sufficient tenderness what here needs to be said?... God, who made these deserving people, may really be right when He thinks that their modest prosperity and the happiness of their children are not enough to make them blessed... And therefore He troubles them, warning them in advance of an insufficiency that one day they will have to discover... This illusion of self-sufficiency may be at its strongest in some very honest, kindly, and temperate people, and on such people, therefore, misfortune must fall.

≈ *THE PROBLEM OF PAIN*

# Mortification

The possibility of pain is inherent in the very existence of a world where souls can meet. When souls become wicked they will certainly use this possibility to hurt one another; and this, perhaps, accounts for four-fifths of the sufferings of men. It is men, not God, who have produced racks, whips, prisons, slavery, guns, bayonets, and bombs; it is by human avarice or human stupidity, not by the churlishness of nature, that we have poverty and overwork. But there remains, none the less, much suffering which cannot thus be traced to ourselves. Even if all the suffering were man-made, we should like to know the reason for the enormous permission to torture their fellows which God gives to the worst of men...

To surrender a self-will inflamed and swollen with years of usurpation is a kind of death. We all remember this self-will as it was in childhood: the bitter, prolonged rage at every thwarting, the burst of passionate tears, the black, Satanic wish to kill or die rather than to give in... And if, now that we are grown up, we do not howl and stamp quite so much, that is partly because our elders

*The Rider of Strife,* HENRI EMILIEN ROUSSEAU (1875–1933)

began the process of breaking or killing our self-will in the nursery, and partly because the same passions now take more subtle forms and have grown clever at avoiding death by various 'compensations'. Hence the necessity to die daily: however often we think we have broken the rebellious self we shall still find it alive. That this process cannot be without pain is sufficiently witnessed by the very history of the word 'mortification'.

≈ *THE PROBLEM OF PAIN*

# The lifting
# of the sorrow

For various reasons, not in themselves at all mysterious, my heart was lighter than it had been for many weeks. For one thing, I suppose I am recovering physically from a good deal of mere exhaustion. And I'd had a very tiring but very healthy twelve hours the day before, and a sounder night's sleep; and after ten days of low-hung grey skies and motionless warm dampness, the sun was shining and there was a light breeze. And suddenly at the very moment when, so far, I mourned H. least, I remembered her best. Indeed it was something (almost) better than memory; an instantaneous, unanswerable impression. To say it was like a meeting would be going too far. Yet there was that

in it which tempts one to use those words. It was as if the lifting of the sorrow removed a barrier…

Such was the fact. And I believe I can make sense out of it. You can't see anything properly while your eyes are blurred with tears. You can't, in most things, get what you want if you want it too desperately: anyway, you can't get the best out of it. 'Now! Let's have a real good talk' reduces everyone to silence, 'I *must* get a good sleep tonight' ushers in hours of wakefulness. Delicious drinks are wasted on a really ravenous thirst. Is it similarly the very intensity of the longing that draws the iron curtain, that makes us feel we are staring into a vacuum when we think about our dead? 'Them as asks' (at any rate, 'as asks too importunately') don't get. Perhaps can't.

≈ *A GRIEF OBSERVED*

*No. 126,* TREVOR NEAL

# Our failures
# are forgiven

Chastity is the most unpopular of the Christian virtues. There is no getting away from it: the Christian rule is, 'Either marriage, with complete faithfulness to your partner, or else total abstinence.' Now this is so difficult and so contrary to our instincts, that obviously either Christianity is wrong or our sexual instinct, as it now is, has gone wrong. One or the other. Of course, being a Christian, I think it is the instinct which has gone wrong...

We may, indeed, be sure that perfect chastity – like perfect charity – will not be attained by any merely human efforts. You must ask for God's help. Even when you have done so, it may seem to you for a long time that no help, or less help than you need, is being given. Never mind. After each failure, ask forgiveness,

pick yourself up, and try again. Very often what God first helps us towards is not the virtue itself but just this power of always trying again. For however important chastity (or courage, or truthfulness, or any other virtue) may be, this process trains us in habits of the soul which are more important still. It cures our illusions about ourselves and teaches us to depend on God. We learn, on the one hand, that we cannot trust ourselves even in our best moments, and, on the other, that we need not despair even in our worst, for our failures are forgiven. The only fatal thing is to sit down content with anything less than perfection.

≈ *MERE CHRISTIANITY*

# A horror to God

The emotion of shame has been valued not as an emotion but because of the insight to which it leads. I think that insight should be permanent in each man's mind: but whether the painful emotions that attend it should also be encouraged, is a technical problem of spiritual direction on which, as a layman, I have little call to speak. My own idea, for what it is worth, is that all sadness which is not either arising from the repentance of a concrete sin and hastening towards concrete amendment or restitution, or else arising from pity and hastening to active assistance, is simply bad; and I think we all sin by needlessly disobeying the apostolic injunction to 'rejoice' as much as by anything else. Humility, after the first shock, is a cheerful virtue: it is the high-minded unbeliever, desperately trying in the teeth of repeated disillusions to retain his 'faith in human nature', who is really sad...

I have been trying to make the reader believe that we actually are, at present, creatures whose character must be, in some respects, a horror to God, as it is, when we

*Sandwich Man,* COLIN WILLIAM MOSS (B.1914)

really see it, a horror to ourselves. This I believe to be a fact: and I notice that the holier a man is, the more fully aware he is of that fact. Perhaps you have imagined that this humility in the saints is a pious illusion at which God smiles. That is a most dangerous error... It is practically dangerous because it encourages a man to mistake his first insights into his own corruption for the first beginnings of a halo around his own silly head. No; depend upon it, when the saints say that they – even they – are vile, they are recording truth with scientific accuracy.

≈ *THE PROBLEM OF PAIN*

# Surrender and humiliation

The perfect surrender and humiliation were undergone by Christ; perfect because He was God, surrender and humiliation because He was man. Now the Christian belief is that if we somehow share the humility and suffering of Christ we shall also share in His conquest of death and find a new life after we have died... People often ask when the next step in evolution – the step to something beyond man – will happen. But in the Christian view, it has happened already. In Christ a new kind of man appeared: and the new kind of life which began in Him is to be put into us...

Your natural life is derived from your parents; that does not mean it will stay there if you do nothing about it.

*Christ Taken Captive,*
HIERONYMUS BOSCH (c.1450–1516)

You can lose it by neglect, or you can drive it away by committing suicide. You have to feed it and look after it: but always remember you are not making it, you are only keeping up a life you got from someone else. In the same way a Christian can lose the Christ-life which has been put into him, and he has to make efforts to keep it… As long as the natural life is in your body, it will do a lot towards repairing that body. Cut it, and up to a point it will heal, as a dead body would not. A live body is not one that never gets hurt, but one that can to some

extent repair itself. In the same way a Christian is not a man who never goes wrong, but a man who is enabled to repent and pick himself up and begin over again after each stumble – because the Christ-life is inside him, repairing him all the time, enabling him to repeat (in some degree) the kind of voluntary death which Christ Himself carried out.

≈ *MERE CHRISTIANITY*

# Too perfect to last

I think I am beginning to understand why grief feels like suspense. It comes from the frustration of so many impulses that had become habitual. Thought after thought, feeling after feeling, had H. for their object. Now their target is gone. I keep on through habit fitting an arrow to the string; then I remember and have to lay the bow down. So many roads lead thought to H. I set out on one of them. But now there's an impassable frontier post across it. So many roads once; now so many *culs-de-sac...*

*Tibet Sunrise*, RUSSELL JOHNSON

'It was too perfect to last,' so I am tempted to say of our marriage. But it can be meant in two ways. It may be grimly pessimistic – as if God no sooner saw two of His creatures happy than He stopped it ('None of that here!'). As if He were like the hostess at the sherry party who separates two guests the moment they show signs of having got into a real conversation. But it could also mean 'This had reached its proper perfection. This had become what it had in it to be. Therefore of course it would not be prolonged.' As if God said, 'Good; you have mastered that exercise. I am very pleased with it. And now you are ready to go on to the next.' When you have learned to do quadratics and enjoy doing them you will not be set them much longer. The teacher moves you on.

≈ *A GRIEF OBSERVED*

# The poison
# of hate-in-love

E ros is notoriously the most mortal of our loves. The world rings with complaints of his fickleness. What is baffling is the combination of this fickleness with his protestations of permanency. To be in love is both to intend and to promise lifelong fidelity. Love makes vows unasked; can't be deterred from making them. 'I will be ever true,' are almost the first words he utters. Not hypocritically but sincerely...

The event of falling in love is of such a nature that we are right to reject as intolerable the idea that it should be transitory. In one high bound it has overleaped the massive wall of our selfhood; it has made appetite itself altruistic, tossed personal happiness aside as a triviality and planted the interests of another in the centre of our being. Spontaneously and without effort we have fulfilled the law (towards one person) by loving our neighbour as ourselves. It is an image, a foretaste, of what we must become to all if Love Himself rules in us without a rival...

*Youth with Arrow,* GIORGIONE (1477/78–1510)

Eros needs help; therefore needs to be ruled. The god dies or becomes a demon unless he obeys God. But he may live on, mercilessly chaining together two mutual tormentors, each raw all over with the poison of hate-in-love, each ravenous to receive and implacably refusing to give, jealous, determined to be free and to allow no freedom, living on 'scenes'... The lovers' old hyperbole of 'eating' each other can come horribly near to the truth.

≈ *THE FOUR LOVES*

# No one minds about me at all

'I forgive him as a Christian,' said the Ghost. 'But there are some things one can never forget... You haven't the faintest conception of what I went through with your dear Robert. The ingratitude! It was I who made a man of him! Sacrificed my whole life to him!... I used to spend simply *hours* arranging flowers to make that poky little house nice... and there was a perfectly frightful fuss one evening because I'd spilled one of the vases over some papers of his. It was all nonsense really, because they weren't anything to do with his work. He had some silly idea of writing a book in those days... as if he could. I cured him of that in the end...

*Dreams of the Past, Hampton Court,*
ADELAIDE CLAXTON (FL. 1860–76)

'The trouble I went to entertaining! Robert's idea was that he'd just slink off by himself every now and then to see what he called his old friends… "No, Robert," I said, "your friends are now mine. It is my duty to have them *here*, however tired I am and however little we can afford it."…

'And then, he got the new job. A great step up. But… all he said was "Well *now*, for God's sake let's have some peace."… I nearly gave him up altogether: but I knew my duty… I *forced* him to take exercise… I kept on giving parties… Even, when things became desperate, I encouraged him to take up his writing again. It couldn't do any harm by then. How could I help it if he *did* have a nervous breakdown in the end? My conscience is clear…

'No, Hilda, listen. Please, please! I'm so miserable. I must have someone to – to do things to. It's simply frightful down here. No one minds about me at all. I can't alter them…'

≈ *THE GREAT DIVORCE*

# The fatal flaw

Would I be safe in guessing that every second person has in his life a terrible problem, conditioned by some other person; either someone you work for, or someone who works for you, either someone among your friends or your relations, or actually someone in your own house, who is making, and has for years made, your life very much more difficult than it need be? – someone who has that fatal flaw in his character, on which again and again all your efforts have been wrecked, someone whose fatal laziness or jealousy or intolerable temper, or the fact that he never tells the truth, or the fact that he will always backbite and bear tales, or whatever the fatal flaw may be, which, whether it breaks him or not, will certainly break you...

When God looks into your office, or parish, or school, or hospital, or factory, or home, He sees all these people like that, and of course, sees one more, the one whom you do not see. For we may be quite certain that, just as in other people… so in us there is something equally fatal, on which their endeavours have again and again been shipwrecked…

A serious attempt to repent and really to know one's own sins is in the long run a lightening and relieving process. Of course, there is bound to be at first dismay and often terror and later great pain, yet that is much less in the long run than the anguish of a mass of unrepented and unexamined sins, lurking in the background of our minds.

≈ 'MISERABLE OFFENDERS'

# War makes death real

War threatens us with death and pain. No man ... need try to attain a stoic indifference about these things: but we can guard against the illusions of the imagination. We think of the streets of Warsaw and contrast the deaths there suffered with an abstraction called Life. But there is no question of death or life for any of us; only a question of this death or of that – of a machine gun bullet now or a cancer forty years later. What does war do to death? It certainly does not make it more frequent: 100 per cent of us die, and the percentage cannot be increased. It puts several deaths earlier: but I hardly suppose that that is what we fear.

*Wartime Oxford*

Certainly when the moment comes, it will make little difference how many years we have behind us. Does it increase our chances of a painful death? I doubt it... what we call natural

death is usually preceded by suffering: and a battlefield is one of the very few places where one has a reasonable prospect of dying with no pain at all. Does it increase our chances of dying at peace with God? I cannot believe it. If active service does not persuade a man to prepare for death, what ... would? Yet war does do something to death. It forces us to remember it... War makes death real to us: and that would have been regarded as one of its blessings by most of the great Christians of the past.

*Barbed Wire,*
LOUIS RAEMAEKERS (1896–1956)

≈ 'LEARNING IN WAR-TIME'

# Animal pain

*Fate of the Animals*, FRANZ MARC (1880–1916)

The problem of animal suffering is appalling; not because the animals are so numerous (for... no more pain is felt when a million suffer than when one suffers) but because the Christian explanation of human pain cannot be extended to animal pain. So far as we know, beasts are incapable either of sin or virtue: therefore they can neither deserve pain nor be improved by it. At the same time we must never allow the problem of animal suffering to become the centre of the problem of pain; not because it is unimportant – whatever furnishes plausible grounds for questioning the goodness

of God is very important indeed – but because it is outside the range of our knowledge. God has given us data which enable us, in some degree, to understand our own suffering: He has given us no such data about beasts. We know neither why they were made nor what they are, and everything we say about them is speculative. From the doctrine that God is good we may confidently deduce that the *appearance* of reckless Divine cruelty in the animal kingdom is an illusion – and the fact that the only suffering we know at first hand (ours) turns out not to be a cruelty will make it easier to believe this. After that, everything is guesswork…

We have reason to believe that not all animals suffer as we think they do: but some, at least, look as if they had selves, and what shall be done for these innocents? And we have seen that it is possible to believe that animal pain is not God's handiwork but begun by Satan's malice and perpetuated by man's desertion of his post: still, if God has not caused it, He has permitted it, and, once again, what shall be done for these innocents?

≈ *THE PROBLEM OF PAIN*

# The pain is not the whole thing

I have just got your letter of the 22nd containing the sad news of your father's death. But, dear lady, I hope you and your mother are not really trying to pretend it didn't happen. It does happen, happens to all of us, and I have no patience with the high-minded people who make out that it 'doesn't matter'. It matters a great deal, and very solemnly. And for those who are left, the pain is not the whole thing. I feel very strongly (and I am not alone in this) that some great good comes from the dead to the living in the months or weeks after the death. I think I was much helped by my own father after his death: as if Our Lord welcomed the newly dead with the gift of some power to bless those they have left behind... Certainly they often seem just at that time to be very near us.

≈ *LETTERS OF C.S. LEWIS*

# I feel very much an orphan

And do you pray for me, especially at present when I feel very much an orphan because my aged confessor and most loving father in Christ has just died. While he was celebrating at the altar, suddenly, after a most sharp but (thanks be to God) very brief attack of pain, he expired; and his last words were, 'I come, Lord Jesus'. He was a man of ripe spiritual wisdom – noble minded but of an almost childlike simplicity and innocence.

≈ *LATIN LETTERS*

# This Vale of Tears

I grieve and condole with you at the death of a most dearly loved friend. He, indeed, from the troubles of this world which he used to feel most heavily, has happily passed over into his own Country; to you without doubt the grief is keen...

It was good of you, reverend Father, to send me this most beautiful book about the life of dearest Father John. I thank you. I hope that from reading this book I shall become better informed about many things which till now have remained obscure; for often this holy man in his letters implied that he laboured under I know not what secret grief, in the hidden counsels of God who chastises everyone whom He receives as a son...

Be assured that your House is daily named in my prayers. And do you persevere in prayers for us. For now, after two years' remission, my wife's mortal illness has returned. May it please the Lord that, whatever is His will for the body, the minds of both of us may remain unharmed; that faith unimpaired may strengthen us, contrition soften us and peace make us joyful...

I know that you pour forth your prayers both for my most dearly-longed-for wife and also for me who – now bereaved and as it were halved – journey on, through this Vale of Tears, alone.

≈ *LATIN LETTERS*

# The cure of death is dying

Within an inch of him he had seen a face. Now a cloud crossed the moon and the face was no longer visible, but he knew that it was still looking at him – an aged, appalling face, crumbling and chaotic, larger than human. Presently its voice began.

'Do you still think it is the black hole you fear? Do you not know even now the deeper fear whereof the black hole is the veil? Do you not know why they would all persuade you that there is nothing beyond the brook and that when a man's lease is out his story is done? Because, if this were true, they could in their reckoning make me equal to nought, therefore not dreadful... They have prophesied soft things to you. I am no negation, and the deepest of your heart acknowledges it. Else why have you buried the memory of your uncle's face so carefully that it has needed all these things to bring it up? Do not think that you can escape me; do not think you can call me Nothing. To you I am not Nothing; I am the being blindfolded, the losing all power of self-

*Camille Monet on her Deathbed*, CLAUDE MONET (1840–1926)

defence, the surrender, not because any terms are offered, but because resistance is gone: the step into the dark... The Landlord's Son who feared nothing, feared me.'

'What am I to do?' said John.

'Which you choose,' said the voice. 'Jump, or be thrown... Give in or struggle.'

'I would sooner do the first, if I could.'

'Then I am your servant and no more your master. The cure of death is dying. He who lays down his liberty in that act receives it back...'

≈ *THE PILGRIM'S REGRESS*

# Acknowledgements

The Editor and Publishers are grateful for permission to use the following
material, which is reproduced by permission of the copyright holders:
*The Four Loves*, *The Great Divorce*, *Mere Christianity*, *Letters of C.S. Lewis*, *The
Pilgrim's Regress*, *Poems*, *Prayer: Letters to Malcolm*, *The Problem of Pain* and
*Surprised By Joy*, and the essays 'Learning in War-Time' and 'Miserable
Offenders' are reproduced by kind permission of HarperCollins*Publishers*.
*A Grief Observed* by kind permission of Faber & Faber.
*They Stand Together* by kind permission of Curtis Brown Ltd.
*Latin Letters* by kind permission of Curtis Brown Ltd and, for his
translation from the Latin, Mr Martin Moynihan.
All items are the copyright of C.S. Lewis Pte Ltd.

Full details of the writings of C.S. Lewis can be found in *C.S. Lewis:
A Companion and Guide*, by Walter Hooper, published by
HarperCollins*Publishers*, in 1996.

Cover Hulton Deutsch Collection/John Chillingworth

AKG London: p 21 (Alte Pinakothek, Munich), 23 (Musée du Louvre),
49 (Kunsthistorisches Museum, Vienna); Chris Beetles (Arthur Hunt):
pp 16/17, 26/27, 60/61; Bridgeman Art Library: pp 2, 28 (both Alte
Pinakothek, Munich). 11 (City Museum & Art Gallery, Stoke-on-
Trent/Courtesy of David Shepherd), 13 (Wallace Collection, London),
15 (Christie's Images), 21 (Courtesy of the Bundanon Trust, Australia),
24/25 (Atkinson Art Gallery, Southport, Lancs), 30 (National Gallery,
London), 33 (Guildhall Art Gallery, London), 34 (Harris Museum & Art
Gallery, Preston), 37 (Musée d'Orsay, Paris), 38/39 (Private Collection),
43 (Private Collection), 44/45 (San Diego Museum of Art),
50 (Private Collection), 55 (Stapleton Collection), 56/57 (Öffentliche
Kunstsammlung, Basle). 63 (Musée d'Orsay, Paris); ILN Picture Library:
pp 8 bottom; The Marion E. Wade Center, Wheaton, Illinois:
pp 6 inset, 7 inset, 18; 31; Tibet Images: p 46